Locke

by

MAURICE CRANSTON

Published for The British Council
and The National Book League
by Longmans, Green & Co.

Two shillings and

"Locke" says Mr. Cranston "set men on the road to the greatest possible liberty by the method he used to set them on the road to the greatest possible knowledge—by teaching them the impossibility of the absolute." His assessment of this important philosopher and man of affairs includes an appreciation of all Locke's principal works. Mr. Cranston's longer study of Locke, largely based upon material recently acquired by the Bodleian Library, appeared in 1957. It was awarded the James Tait Black Memorial Prize. He wrote the booklet on *John Stuart Mill* which appears as No. 99 in this Series.

Bibliographical Series
of Supplements to 'British Book News'
on Writers and their Work

*

GENERAL EDITOR
Bonamy Dobrée

JOHN LOCKE

from a portrait by Sir Godfrey Kneller
in the Frick Art Reference Library, New York,
reproduced by kind permission

LOCKE

by
MAURICE CRANSTON

PUBLISHED FOR
THE BRITISH COUNCIL
and the NATIONAL BOOK LEAGUE
by LONGMANS, GREEN & CO.

LONGMANS, GREEN & CO. LTD.
48 Grosvenor Street, London W.1
Thibault House, Thibault Square, Cape Town
605–611 Lonsdale Street, Melbourne C.1.

LONGMANS, GREEN & CO. INC.
119 West 40th Street, New York 18

LONGMANS, GREEN & CO.
20 Cranfield Road, Toronto 16

ORIENT LONGMANS PRIVATE LTD.
Calcutta Bombay Madras
Delhi Hyderabad Dacca

First Published in 1961
© Maurice Cranston 1961

Printed in Great Britain by
F. Mildner & Sons, London, E.C.1

CONTENTS

¶ JOHN LOCKE was born at Wrington, Somerset on 29 August 1632. He died on 28 October 1704 at High Laver, Essex.

LOCKE

I

JOHN LOCKE was a handsome man; the portraits by Greenhill, Kneller and Verelst all depict a sensitive, fastidious, patrician face; the lineaments, one would think, of a poet. And there one would think wrongly. For Locke was many other things—economist, diplomatist, theologian, traveller, scientist, physician, pedagogue as well as philosopher; but he was never a man of artistic and literary taste. David Hume was once said to have looked like 'a turtle-eating alderman instead of a refined philosopher'; Locke, who had the looks Hume lacked, wrote like a water-drinking local councillor, his style ungainly, his idioms commercial, his imagination puritanical, his humour laboured, his interests wholly practical. 'What is the *use*', he asked, 'of poetry?'

He was a great materialist, in a sense, and an important sense. Our modern Western world has been made by scientists, merchants, statesmen, industrialists; Locke was the first philosopher to expound their view of life, to articulate their aspirations and justify their deeds. No philosopher has exercised a greater influence. And yet it could be said—and has been said—that Locke was not a philosopher at all. But to say this is only to say that Locke was not a metaphysician; and he was certainly not one, in the sense that Leibniz or Spinoza, his contemporaries, were metaphysicians. Locke offered no all-embracing system to explain the nature of the universe. On the contrary, he tried to show that the human understanding is so limited that such comprehensive knowledge is beyond men's powers to reach. Where philosophy is concerned Locke did not give the answers; he achieved greatness rather in his formulation of the problems. He set out, as no one had done before, the questions philosophy should deal with, and also the ways of dealing with them; he gave epistemology, the theory of knowledge, its method.

7

Two powerful streams in seventeenth century thought, the semi-sceptical rational theorising of Descartes, and the *ad hoc* scientific experimenting of Bacon and the Royal Society came together in Locke. Their union was not perfect, because the streams were so different, but his mind was the meeting point, a point which marked a new beginning, not only in philosophy, but in the way in which men thought about the world. Locke, one might almost say, had the first modern mind. Descartes, though more original than Locke, was still in many ways a medieval thinker; his philosophy was still attached to theology. Even Gassendi, who anticipated much of Locke, did not quite leap free. Locke made the break; he separated philosophy from theology, and set the proper study of philosophy within the boundaries of man's experience: 'Our portion', he wrote, 'lies only here in this little spot of earth, where we and all our concernments are shut up.'

Yet Locke was not a sceptic, and in his capacity as theologian he had thoughts of his own about God to expound. He quarrelled with bishops and the orthodox of most denominations. He maintained that a Christian need believe no more than the single proposition 'that Christ is the Messiah'; but to that minimal creed he clung with the firmest assurance. He had a quiet and steady faith in the immortality of the soul, and in the prospects of happiness in the life to come. He had no belief in miracles, and no patience with people who had mystical experiences or visions of God, and he detested religious enthusiasm, but in his own unemotional way he was, like Newton, a deeply religious man.

II

John Locke was born on 29 August, 1632, at Wrington in Somerset. His grandfather, Nicholas Locke, was a successful clothier of that county. His father, John Locke, was a less prosperous lawyer and clerk to the local magistrates. His mother came from a family of tanners; she was aged 35 when the future philosopher, her first child, was born; her husband was only 26. The baby was baptised at Wrington by Samuel Crook, one of the leading Calvinist intellectuals of the West of England; and brought up in an atmosphere of austerity and discipline. The Civil War broke out when Locke was ten years old, and his father was mounted as a captain of Parliamentary Horse by Alexander Popham, a rich local magistrate turned Colonel. Apart from demolishing some Popish images in Wells cathedral, the two officers saw little action, but a grateful Alexander Popham became the patron of his captain's eldest son, and when a few years later Westminster School was taken over by the Parliament, the colonel found a place for his protégé in what was then the best boarding school in the country.

At Westminster Locke came under the influence of the Royalist headmaster Richard Busby, whom the Parliamentary governors had imprudently allowed to remain in charge of the school; and when Locke left in 1652 to become an undergraduate at Christ Church, Oxford, he was well prepared to react against the rule of the Calvinist 'saints' which then prevailed in the university. By 1659 Locke had become a right-wing Monarchist; by 1661 his political views were close to those of Thomas Hobbes. It was at this time he wrote his first political pamphlet. Locke's Victorian biographer, H. R. Fox Bourne, who is generally reliable although he had no access to the large collection of Locke papers which Lord Lovelace sold to the Bodleian Library in 1948, spread abroad the idea that Locke was a life-long liberal. Finding liberal sentiments expressed in a manuscript entitled *Reflections on the Roman Commonwealth* and dated 1661, Fox Bourne concluded that Locke 'had already arrived at conclusions in political science from which he never greatly swerved'. In fact, Locke did not write the *Reflections on the Roman Commonwealth*. The real author was a man named Walter Moyle. Locke *did* write on politics in

1661, but the sentiments he expressed were by no means liberal ones.

Locke in 1661 was a newly elected Christ Church don, and one of his political papers was written as an answer to a pamphlet by another Student of the same college—*The Great Question Concerning Things Indifferent in Religious Worship*, by Edward Bagshawe. Bagshawe argued that where the commands of God were not specific, the state should leave men free to worship as they pleased. His pamphlet was a plea for toleration. Locke's reply was a polemic against toleration. He maintained that the civil ruler 'must necessarily have an absolute and arbitrary power over all the indifferent actions of his people'. His argument was based on the proposition that men were born by God's design 'subject to the will and pleasure of another', namely to the will and pleasure of their civil ruler.

In a preface to this pamphlet against Bagshawe, Locke said that 'there is no one who can have a greater respect and veneration for authority than I'. He recalled that he had been born in 'a storm', a political storm which had 'lasted almost hitherto', and he confessed that the calm which the Restoration of Charles II had brought with it was so welcome to him that he felt obliged in duty and in gratitude to encourage 'obedience'.

The influence of Hobbes, which was considerable throughout Locke's life, though Locke never admitted it, was at this period most pronounced. Locke's pamphlet was intended for publication, but it was not published; it has never yet been published. Other controversialists went more swiftly into print and achieved Locke's object. Bagshawe was expelled from his Studentship of Christ Church, and the Anglican majority in Parliament firmly resisted all pleas for religious toleration. A few years later Bagshawe died on bail from Newgate Prison. By that time, however, Locke had ceased to be his adversary; he had begun instead to think as Bagshawe thought.

In the summer of 1666, Locke met and made friends with

Anthony Ashley Cooper, then Lord Ashley, later first Earl of Shaftesbury. 'Shaftesbury' for simplicity's sake I shall call him here. He was not yet the leader of a party, but he was already the outstanding politician of the Left, the most forceful champion of religious toleration. Shaftesbury opposed the Corporation Bill, the Bill of Uniformity, the Five Mile Bill, and every other measure designed to curb the freedom of Nonconformists. He had thus been a spokesman for liberty when Locke still aspired to uphold obedience, but if at the time of their first meeting, Locke had not already come over to Shaftesbury's side, Shaftesbury must soon have pulled him across the last few hurdles.

A year later, at the age of thirty-four, Locke went to live at Shaftesbury's house in London. His Oxford career had not been a particularly distinguished one. He had been a temporary lecturer and a censor at Christ Church, he had made friends with Robert Boyle, one of the founders of the Royal Society, and helped him by collecting scientific data, and he had studied medicine; but he had done no important laboratory work and he had failed to get a medical degree. Even so, it was as a domestic physician that Locke entered Shaftesbury's household, and he soon proved himself an able one. He saved his patron's life, as Shaftesbury believed, when it was threatened by a suppurating cyst of the liver. Afterwards Shaftesbury decided that Locke was far too great a genius to be spending his time on medicine alone, and work of other kinds was found for him.

III

It was under Shaftesbury's patronage that Locke discovered his own true gifts. First he became a philosopher. At Oxford he had been as bored and dissatisfied as Hobbes had been with the medieval Aristotelian philosophy which was taught there. Reading Descartes first opened Locke's

eyes to the 'new philosophy', and discussions with Shaftesbury and other London friends led him to write, in his
fourth year under Shaftesbury's roof, the earliest drafts of
his masterpiece, the *Essay Concerning Human Understanding*.
In London also Locke met Thomas Sydenham, the great
physician, who introduced him to the new clinical method
he had learned in Montpellier. Shaftesbury himself introduced Locke to the study of economics and gave him his
earliest experience of political administration.

Shaftesbury, little, ugly, and vain, has a bad name in the
history books. But he was no fool. He was interested, with
Locke, in philosophy and in science, and he did much to
defend and enlarge the liberties of Englishmen. Admittedly
his concern for religious toleration was prompted less by
Christian forbearance and compassion, than by the belief
that religious persecution divided a nation which would
be stronger and richer if it were united. Shaftesbury was
self-consciously the nationalist and the capitalist. He saw
more clearly than most of his contemporaries that colonial
expansion and international trade might bring at the same
time great fortunes to men like himself and great power to
the country as a whole. He might almost have been invented
by Marx.

When Shaftesbury pleaded for religious toleration he
wished to have it primarily on behalf of Protestant dissenters.
Charles II, who favoured religious toleration primarily for
the sake of Catholic recusants, was for some time in agree-
ment with him against the intolerant Anglican majority.
This was the position in the earliest years of Locke's connection with Shaftesbury. Shaftesbury was then anti-Dutch.
He had studied Holland closely, and his kind of liberal
imperialism was largely based on the Dutch model. He saw
Holland as England's greatest rival in trade and therefore
her greatest potential enemy. Later Shaftesbury came to
regard France, not Holland, in this light, and he altered his
policy accordingly. As Charles II was pro-French this
change put Shaftesbury into opposition, but it also gave

him a principle besides trade and toleration on which to take his public stand. That principle was the Protestant religion. France was Catholic, and everything Catholic served the interests of France; France was England's natural enemy, therefore everything Catholic was inimical to England's interests. The case was easily argued, though indeed it hardly needed to be argued. The very name of 'Popery' was enough to agitate the public.

Shaftesbury, however, liked to argue; he liked to be able to express his ideas in theoretical terms; and as his physician was also a philosopher, he invited Locke to reflect on the general principles involved in these matters of political expediency. Was it illogical to stand both for religious toleration and for the suppression of Catholics? Locke came to the conclusion that it was not. Catholics were just not religious dissenters, they were a body of men who acknowledged allegiance to a foreign potentate, the Pope, and who were therefore allied through Rome with the Pope's true friends, the French, No country, Locke believed, could tolerate within it people who were potentially disloyal. It was not a question of religious liberty, but of the security of the realm, and the defence of the realm was the first duty of any government.

Locke stayed with Shaftesbury on and off until Shaftesbury's death in 1682. In those fifteen years Shaftesbury's Protestant zeal carried him to the point of organizing a rebellion. Charles II refused to deny his Catholic brother, James, his legitimate right to succeed him to the throne. Shaftesbury persuaded Parliament to pass a measure designed to make James's succession illegal. When Charles thwarted this manoeuvre, Shaftesbury replied by calling on his friends to rise and exclude James in favour of a Protestant successor by force of arms. The Protestant successor he unwisely named was Charles's bastard, Monmouth. But his supporters hesitated, the plot was nipped, and he himself withdrew to Holland, there, soon afterwards, to die.

These were the events which stand behind Locke's *Two*

Treatises of Civil Government. The book was not published until eight years after Shaftesbury's death, by which time Englishmen had come round to Shaftesbury's way of thinking to the extent of taking up arms to expel James II and enthroning his Protestant nephew, William. Locke in the preface of the published version of his book said he hoped it would 'help to justify the title of King William to rule us'. But Locke had conceived the book, and written most of it, when Charles II was still alive, and when the question of whether a nation had the right to rebel against its ruler was not a backward-looking moral problem but a forward-looking moral challenge.

Textbooks of political science, having said their piece about its being intended to justify William, usually go on to describe the *Civil Government* as if it were a critique of Hobbes, a philosophical book written in reply to the *Leviathan* and *De Cive*. In fact the *Civil Government* belongs to the literature of persuasion and the greater part of it was written in reply to Sir Robert Filmer's *Patriarcha*.

Filmer was not, as Hobbes was, a man of genius, but he was more important politically at the time because his was the official Tory point of view. Whereas Hobbes recommended obedience on purely selfish and prudential or, as one might say, scientific grounds, Filmer was high-minded and religious. The authority of hereditary monarchs, including the Stuart Kings, derived, he said, from God, and he set out to prove this claim by reference to the Bible. People listened to Filmer because he said what they wanted to hear. And it was because Filmer was influential that Locke chose to answer him.

Locke was not alone in replying to Filmer. In 1681 there was published in London a book entitled *Patriarcha non Monarcha*. The author was James Tyrrell, one of Locke's closest and oldest friends. There is no reference to *Patriarcha non Monarcha* in the *Civil Government*, but there is a striking similarity of argument. Appearing as it did in the reign of Charles II, *Patriarcha non Monarcha* was thoughtfully embellished with a portrait of that king and in the preface there was a note to the effect that the doctrine of absolute sovereignty was something utterly alien to Englishmen. Otherwise the main lines of Tyrrell's argument was almost the same as Locke's in the first of his two treatises on *Civil Government*.

Both Locke and Tyrrell argued that the authority of a father over his children was not absolute, but subject to Natural Law, so that if the authority of Kings over their subjects were derived from the authority of fathers over their children it would not be absolute. Then they both said, with Hobbes, that the authority of kings over their subjects could *not* be derived from the authority of fathers over their children because the relationship of a father to his children was a natural one, which the relationship of a king to his subjects was not. But whereas Tyrrell forbore to elicit the principle that subjects had therefore a right to resist kings who disregard Natural Law, Locke pressed home this conclusion with particular force; and whereas Tyrrell had little to say about the contract theory of the origin of society, Locke dealt with it at length.

The social contract Locke expounded was something very different from that of Hobbes. Locke believed that the social contract had actually taken place. He believed it was a fact of history that men had once lived in a state of natural anarchy and had then banded together to form political societies. For Hobbes the social contract was only an analytic device, an attempt to apply the method of Galileo to the study of civil society.

Locke abandoned the Hobbesian view of the horrors of natural anarchy because he abandoned the Hobbesian view of human nature. Locke in his maturity took a Christian view instead, albeit a Christian view purged of the idea of original sin. Man, according to Locke, was subject, even in a state of nature, to the rule of Natural Law, which was ultimately God's law made known to men through the voice of reason. This is a perplexing suggestion. Hobbes's analysis has the advantages of simplicity: either you are ruled or you are not ruled, either you have liberty or you have obedience, either you have chaos and danger or you have security and fetters. Neither condition is ideal, Hobbes realised, but thought the worst government better than no government at all. The Lockian analysis is more complicated. For Locke believed that men *could* be both ruled and free. Subject in a state of nature to the rule of Natural Law, men were also endowed with Natural Rights—notably the rights to life, liberty, and property—and these rights were retained when men formed political societies. Instead of all *surrendering* equally their liberty to a sovereign as Hobbes suggested, men had in forming political societies merely, according to Locke, *entrusted* power to a sovereign. In return for the advantages of settled justice and mutual security, men had agreed to obey their rulers, but only on condition that their Natural Rights were respected by those rulers. Natural Rights, being rooted in Natural Law, were rooted in something higher than the edicts of princes, they were rooted in the edicts of God. They were inalienable.

Locke's 'right to rebellion'—the right of men to overthrow a ruler who failed to respect the Natural Rights of his subjects—thus derived not only from the idea of the social contract but from the supremacy of God's law to man-made law. People who might have understood, or, understanding, might not have been impressed by the social contract theory, could both appreciate and respond to the principle that God's law is higher than the law of earthly rulers.

Locke met Filmer on Filmer's ground. He championed the rights of men against the rights of kings, and appealed as Filmer did, to the Almighty. Hobbes, for all his quotations from the Bible, was on different ground: the ground of *Realpolitik*, psychology and geometrical method. But the religion Locke appealed to was, in its way, as 'unmedieval' as Hobbes's positivism. It was not the astringent faith of the

Church or of Calvin, but that kind of Christianity both watered down and sweetened which later was known as 'Modernism'.

Had 'Modernist' been a 17th century word, Locke might have been pleased to be called one. The word he would not tolerate was 'Socinian'. He *was* a Socinian, in that his religious opinions were indistinguishable from Socinian opinions, but he protested vigorously that he was not one. When a critic of his, a fighting pamphleteer named Edwards, declared that all Socinians were atheists and that Locke was a Socinian, Locke did not come out against the first of these two propositions, which was false and could be shown to be false, but against the second, and he made very heavy weather of denying what was true. He even protested that he had never read the leading Socinian authors, though his notebooks contain excerpts he had already copied from their writings. Presumably Locke denied this acquaintance with Socinian books from the same motive which prompted him to deny his acquaintance with Hobbes's books. 'Socinian' and 'Hobbist' were both pejorative words, and Locke in his later years was extra- ordinarily anxious to avoid a bad name.

He was never a candid man. He had an almost Gothic fondness of mystery for the sake of mystery: he used all kinds of little cyphers, he modified a shorthand system for the purposes of concealment, and on at least one occasion he employed invisible ink. He guarded his anonymity as an author with elaborate care. He kept secrets from people who were supposed to be his closest friends. 'Do not tell Mr. Oakley' is an injunction which occurs more than once in Locke's letters to Edward Clarke. 'Mr. Oakley' was James Tyrrell. Some of this secrecy was plain good sense, dating from the time when Locke was a political fugitive. Some of it served to add a much-needed touch of romance to Locke's relations with his woman friends, a formidable lot of dons' blue-stocking daughters. But because Locke was sometimes secretive for a good reason and sometimes neurotically secretive and sometimes perhaps secretive simply for fun, it is difficult to make out exactly what he was doing at certain times of his life.

IV

Throughout the years when Shaftesbury's house was his London home, Locke retained his Studentship of Christ Church, though he seldom spent as much as a full term in Oxford. His comings and goings were the subject of speculation. In 1675 he was thought to be after a place as a medical don, but he went to France for three and a half years instead. In 1682, after Shaftesbury's disappearance, Locke seemed once more about to settle down in Oxford, and would probably have done so had not the alleged conspiracy of Shaftesbury's Whig successors to kidnap Charles II and his brother at Rye House precipitated such a feverish witch-hunt that Locke felt it would be unsafe to remain in England. He fled, as Shaftesbury had done, to Amsterdam.

In 1684 Locke was expelled in absence from his Studentship of Christ Church by the King's express command. The following summer, after James's succession to the throne, came Monmouth's abortive rebellion in the West of England, and Locke was named by the English government as one of Monmouth's agents in Holland. He went into hiding as 'Dr. van der Linden', but a few months later his name was removed from the list of wanted men, and he emerged from hiding, though he did not return to England.

Locke's friends in Holland included some of William's English courtiers, but Locke himself was seldom at The Hague. When William and his supporters sailed in 1688 to invade the English coast, Locke complained of ill-health and stayed in Rotterdam. His Swiss friend Jean le Clerc called him '*plutôt timide que courageux*', but the remark was hardly just, for Locke, at the age of fifty-six could reasonably feel that he had had his share of danger. He returned to

London quietly in 1689 in the company of Princess Mary who was to become the Queen.

Jean le Clerc's words have been siezed upon by one or two of Locke's biographers because they can be used to support the theory that Locke had never anything to do with such hazardous activities as revolutionary plots. Their story is that Locke was Shaftesbury's friend and aide while Shaftesbury's actions were constitutional, but not at other times. While Shaftesbury was preparing a rebellion, Locke is supposed to have been a remote and harmless Oxford don. Other Oxford dons were not of this opinion, and at least one in Christ Church believed that Locke had a hand in the Rye House plot, that he was working with Monmouth in Holland, and that he was the author of seditious tracts which had been smuggled into England from Amsterdam. This may have been partly true. Shaftesbury, according to his grandson, had employed Locke 'for his secretest negotiations', and Locke was certainly in close touch with some of the conspirators in Holland, but there is no evidence that he wrote any of the smuggled pamphlets.

While he was in Holland Locke's pen was not idle. Among other things he wrote to his friend Edward Clarke at length on the upbringing of Clarke's son; at such length indeed that the author was eventually able to publish his letters in book form as *Thoughts Concerning Education*. In general Locke was in favour of sternness towards the very young, a sternness which should be relaxed as the children grow old enough to be admitted to the companionship of their parents. He was strongly opposed to corporal punishment, but thought it wrong to indulge the whims of children: 'For if the child must have grapes or sugar-plums when he has a mind to them, rather than make the poor baby cry or be out of humour; why, if he is grown up, must he not be satisfied too, if his desires carry him to wine and women?'

Some of Locke's proposals were more startling. Not only did he believe that children's feet should be washed in cold water in winter, but that they 'should wear shoes so thin that might leak and let in water'. He also recommended that children's meals should be served at irregular hours so that their stomachs should not expect food at particular times. He would deny them fruit altogether as 'something totally unwholesome'.

Locke attacked what he called 'the ordinary method of education', namely the 'charging of children's memories' with rules and principles. He suggested instead that unconscious habits should be bred in children by practice. Manners were better learned by example than by precept, and the intellectual disciplines should be made interesting and attractive. He thought that Latin could be learned like French—not from the study of grammar books, but through the experience of speaking it. He was against the study of Greek, except for those who intended to become professed scholars. For the ordinary gentleman Greek was a waste of labour. As for children writing verses, Locke declared, with more than ordinary fervour:

> I have much more to say, and of more weight, against their making verses, verses of any sort; for if he has no genius to poetry, it is the most unreasonable thing in the world to torment a child, and waste his time about that which can never succeed; and if he have a poetic vein, it is to me the strangest thing in the world that the father should desire or suffer it to be cherished or improved. Methinks the parents should labour to have it stifled and suppressed as much as may be; and I know not what reason a father can have to wish his son a poet, who does not desire to have him bid defiance to all other callings and business; which is not yet the worst of the case, for if he proves a successful rhymer, and gets once the reputation of a wit, I desire it to be considered what company and places he is like to spend his time in, nay, and estate too; for it is very seldom seen that any one discovers mines or gold or silver in Parnassus . . . Poetry and gaming, which usually go together, are alike in this too, that they seldom bring any advantage but to those who have nothing else to live on.

Believing that examples were more important than rules in the education of the young, Locke urged parents to keep their children away from the society of domestic servants, whose ill manners were apt 'horribly to infect children'. He even went so far as to suggest that children should be kept away from schools—even the best schools—where inevitably they fell into the company of undesirable companions. Locke was a loyal enough 'Old Westminster' to admit that a boy might get a better classical education at school, but even so, he would recommend a school only to a father who 'thought it worth while to hazard your son's innocence and virtue for a little Latin and Greek'. Locke was firmly of the opinion that education with a private tutor was far more likely to give a pupil 'a genteel carriage, manly thoughts, and a sense of what is worthy and becoming'. And though he admitted it might sound strange 'in the mouth of a bookish man', he added: 'Learning is the least part of good breeding'.

V

Another thing Locke wrote during his stay in Holland was a travel journal, but because he had no eye for beauty and no sense of history his notes make dismal reading. He would go to great trouble to visit some great cathedral or chateau, and then spend much of his time there working out the exact dimensions. He detested ceremonies and show, which he thought irrational and wasteful, and was clearly pleased to find that one of the best Dutch universities had the most nondescript architecture. It proves 'that knowledge depends not on the stateliness of buildings, etc.'.

'Knowlege' is the word which matters here. For Locke's philistinism was in no sense an aberration. Locke wanted to get away from the imagination, from the vague glamour of medieval things, from unthinking adherence to tradition, from enthusiasm, mysticism, and *gloire;* away from all private, visionary insights and down to the publicly verifi-

able, measurable, plain, demonstrable facts; and this desire
was central to his whole mission as a philosopher and
reformer. His antipathy to imaginative artists was coupled
with contempt for ivory-tower scholars who 'converse
with but one sort of men and read but one sort of books',
and thus:

> canton out to themselves a little goshen in the intellectual world
> where the light shines, and, as they conclude, day blesses them;
> but the rest of that vast *expansum* they give up to night and to
> darkness; and so avoid coming near it. They have a pretty traffic
> with known correspondents in some little creek; within that they
> confine themselves and are dexterous managers enough of the
> wares and products of that corner, but will not venture out into
> the great ocean of knowledge . . .

Venturing out into the great ocean of knowledge made
Locke a polymath, but he was in no sense a smatterer.
Admittedly his expertness was not equally marked in all the
subjects he chose to study. Compared to Boyle and Newton,
who were his friends, Locke was an amateurish scientist; his
knowledge of the Scriptures was questionable; and although
he was an original as well as an influential economist he
could not appreciate the subtlety of other theorists in that
field. What was important in Locke's case, however, was
not his versatility itself, but that each department of knowledge was related in his mind to all the others.

During his exile in Holland he wrote, from drafts he had
made in 1671, his *Essay Concerning Human Understanding*,
his first *Letter for Toleration*, and he may have done some
work on his *Civil Government*. The *Letter for Toleration* was
published in Locke's original Latin at Gouda in 1689, and
an English translation made by the Socinian William
Popple—made, Locke afterwards said, "without my pri-
vity"—was published in London a few months later. The
Human Understanding and the *Civil Government* were also
brought out by different London booksellers in the winter
of 1689-90. Only the *Human Understanding* bore Locke's

name, but its success was so great that it made its author
famous throughout Europe even in his lifetime.

VI

In the Epistle to the Reader, printed at the beginning
of his *Essay Concerning Human Understanding*, Locke says
that in an age of such 'master builders' as Boyle and Sydenham and Huygenius and 'the incomparable Mr. Newton'
it is, for him, 'ambition enough to be employed as an under-
labourer in clearing the ground a little and removing some
of the rubbish that lies in the way of knowledge'. Despite
this modest explanation of his purpose Locke is generally,
and rightly, believed to have done much more. He provides,
among other things, the first modern philosophy of science.
A recurrent word—perhaps the most important word—in
the *Essay* is a Cartesian one, 'idea'. Locke's use of the word
is curious. He does not merely say that we have ideas in our
minds when we think; he says that we have ideas in our
minds when we see, hear, smell, taste, or feel. The core of
his epistemology is the notion that the objects of perception
are not *things*, but ideas which are derived in part from
things in the external world, but which also depend to
some extent on our own minds for their existence. Locke
defines an 'idea' as the 'object of the understanding' whether
it is notion, an entity, or an illusion, perception being for
him a 'species of understanding'.

Locke opens his *Essay* with an attack on what was in his
time the established opinion that certain ideas are innate.
He claims that they have been thought to be innate only
because people cannot remember when they first learned
them. Locke's belief is that we are born in total ignorance,
and that even our theoretical ideas of identity, quantity
and substance are derived from experience. He says that a
child gets ideas of black and white, of sweet and bitter

before and not after it gets an idea of abstract principles such as identity or impossibility. 'The sense at first let in particular ideas, and furnish the yet empty cabinet . . .' Afterwards the mind abstracts these theoretical ideas, and so 'comes to be furnished with ideas and language, the materials about which to exercise the discursive faculty'. In the child's development, 'the use of reason becomes daily more visible as these materials that give it employment increase'.

Locke has thus to defend the belief that everything which he calls an idea is derived from sensation, though he admits that the idea may also be produced by what he calls re-flection—'remembering, considering, reasoning, etc.'. He classifies ideas as simple and complex. Simple ideas are those which the mind receives passively. Complex ideas are pro-duced by the exercise of the mind's own powers. It is in his chapters on 'simple ideas' that Locke sets out the main lines of his theory of perception. Most people, if asked what it is that they see, smell, hear, taste or touch would answer 'things', though they might add 'but sometimes illusions, chimeras, mirages, which are not real things'. They would probably maintain that there are two elements in an act of perception: the observer and the object. Locke differs from this plain view in two respects: first he claims that what we perceive is always an idea, as distinct from a thing; secondly, he claims that there are not two but three elements in perception, the observer, the idea, and the object which the idea represents.

The reasoning which leads Locke to this conclusion is not difficult to appreciate. We look at a penny. We are asked to describe it. It is round, brown, and of modest dimensions. But do we really see just this? We look again and what we see is elliptical, not circular; in some lights it is golden, in others black; close to the eye it is large; seen from afar it is tiny. The actual penny, we are certain, cannot be *both* circular and elliptical, both golden all over and black all over. So we may be led to agree that there must be something which is the one and something which is the other, something which changes, and something which does not change, the elliptical 'penny' we see and the real circular penny, or, in Locke's own words, the 'idea' in the mind of the observer and the material 'body' itself.

Locke's theory of perception is both easily defended and easily attacked. It is easily defended in the twentieth century on the basis of what is said by many physicists about the structure of the universe and by many physiologists about the mechanism of perception. The penny we give a child is something that looks brown, feels warm, tastes sharp on the tongue. The penny we give to the scientist is described as a congeries of electrons and protons. He tells us that certain light-waves strike the retina of the observer's eye, while waves of other kinds strike nerve terminals of other sorts: and these processes produce those modifications of the neurological system which we call 'seeing', 'feeling' or 'tasting' a penny. Neither the electrons nor the protons, neither the waves outside nor the modifications inside are brown or warm or astringent. The scientist thus eliminates what Locke called the *secondary* qualities—colour, taste, sound; and these are precisely those qualities which Locke said depended for their existence on the mind of the observer. At the same time, science seems to accept the objective existence of the qualities which Locke called *primary*, and which he thought of as belonging to material bodies themselves: namely impenetrability, extension, figure, mobility and number. These are the qualities with which scientists are accustomed to deal. Nor is Locke's distinction between primary and secondary qualities acceptable only to scientists. Most people would probably be willing to agree that they could imagine an object divested one by one of its qualities of taste and smell and so forth, but they could not imagine a body divested of impenetrability, or shape or size or position in space: for a body without primary qualities would not exist at all.

But if there is much to be said for Locke's epistemology,

there is also much to be said against it. If we are aware in our perceptual experience only of ideas which represent objects, and never of objects themselves, there can be no means of knowing what, if anything, is represented by those ideas. The human predicament, according to Locke's account of it, is that of a man permanently imprisoned in a sort of diving bell, receiving some signals from without and some from within his apparatus, but having no means of knowing which, if any, of these signals come from outside and hence no means of testing the authenticity of any of the signals. Man cannot therefore have any definite knowledge whatever of the external world.

In the later chapters of the *Essay* the author puts an even heavier emphasis on human ignorance. Our knowledge, Locke says, 'is not only limited to the paucity and imperfections of the ideas we have, and which we employ about it', it is something still more circumscribed. Our knowledge of identity and diversity in ideas extends only as far as our ideas themselves; our knowledge of their co-existence extends only a little way because knowledge of any necessary connection between primary and secondary qualities is unattainable. However, with the area of certainty thus diminished, Locke does not deny us the possibility of an assurance which falls short of perfect knowledge. We can have *probable* knowledge; even when we cannot have certain knowledge. Moreover, unlike most of his successors among empiricist philosophers, Locke admits the existence of substance. He says that substance is somehow present in all things, even though we do not see or feel it. What we see and feel are the primary and secondary qualities. Substance is what stands under and props up those qualities. Beyond that Locke says the subject must necessarily remain a mystery: 'It seems probable to me that the simple ideas we receive from sensation and reflection are the boundaries of our thoughts; beyond which the mind, whatever efforts it would make, is not able to advance one jot, nor can it make any discoveries, when it would pry into the nature and hidden causes of those ideas.'

The *Essay Concerning Human Understanding* is a very English book both in its merits and its faults. Its tone is at once moral and pragmatic, its style is homely rather than elegant, its construction informal and even amateurish. The 'pursuit of Truth' the author says, 'is a duty we owe to God . . . and a duty we owe also to ourselves'; utility is at one with piety. Truth, as Locke defines it, is the 'proper riches and furniture of the mind'; but he does not claim to have added to that stock, but rather to have shown the conditions under which the mind could acquire its proper riches and furniture:

> We have no reason to complain that we do not know the nature of the sun or the stars, that the consideration of light itself leaves us in the dark and a thousand other speculations in nature, since, if we knew them, they would be of no solid advantage, nor help to make our lives the happier, they being but the useless employment of idle or over-curious brains . . .
>
> If we will consider man as in the world, and that his mind and faculties were given him for any use, we must necessarily conclude it must be to procure him the happiness which this world is capable of . . . Apart from the next world, we need trouble our heads with nothing but the history of nature and an enquiry into the quality of the things in the mansion of the universe, and being well skilled in the knowledge of material causes and effect of things in our power, directing our thoughts to the improvement of such arts and inventions, engines and utensils as might best contribute to our conveniency and delight.

Locke's general philosophy has obvious implications for a theory of morals. The traditional view in Locke's time was that some sort of moral knowledge was innate in the human person. Locke thought otherwise. What God—or Nature—had given men was a faculty of reason and a sentiment of self-love. Reason in combination with self-love produced morality. Reason could discern the general principles of ethics, or Natural Law, and self-love should lead men to obey those principles. Locke wrote in one of his notebooks:

> Thus I think—it is a man's proper business to seek happiness and avoid misery. Happiness consists in what delights and contents the mind; misery is what disturbs, discomposes, or torments it. I will therefore make it my business to seek satisfaction and delight and avoid uneasiness and disquiet and to have as much of the one and as little of the other as may be. But here I must take care I mistake not, for if I prefer a short pleasure to a lasting one, it is plain I cross my own happiness.
>
> Let me see then wherein consist the most lasting pleasures of this life: and that so far as I can observe is in these things: First, Health, without which no sensual pleasure can have any relish. Secondly, Good Reputation, for that I find everybody is pleased with, and the want of it a torment. Thirdly, Knowledge, for the little knowledge that I have, I find I would not sell at any rate, nor part with for any pleasure. Fourthly, Doing Good. I find the well-cooked meat I ate today does now no more delight me; nay, I am diseased after a full meal. The perfumes I smelt yesterday now no more affect me with any pleasure. But the good turn I did yesterday, a year, seven years hence, continues still to please me as often as I reflect upon it. Fifthly, the expectation of eternal and incomprehensible happiness in another world also carries a constant pleasure with it. If then, I will faithfully pursue that happiness that I propose to myself, whatever pleasure offers itself to me, I must carefully look that it cross not any of these five great and constant pleasures mentioned.

For Locke, in other words, Christian ethics was Natural ethics. The teaching of the New Testament was a means to an end—happiness in this life and in the life to come. Loving one's neighbour and otherwise obeying the precepts of the Saviour was a way to that end. The reason for doing what Christ said was not simply that Christ had said it; there was the additional reason, that by doing these things one promoted one's happiness. There was no need to ask why anyone should desire happiness; because all men were impelled by their natural self-love to desire it.

Wrong doing was thus for Locke a sign of ignorance. People did not always realise that long-term happiness could usually only be bought at the cost of short-term pleasures. Folly drove them to destroy their own well-being. If people were enlightened, if they used their own powers of reason, they would be good; if they were prudent, reflective, calculating, instead of being moved by the transitory winds of impulse and emotion, they would have what they most desired. There is perhaps in this system of morals something rather naïve and commonplace; but then it must be said of Locke that he was in many ways very ordinary as a thinker; but his was an inspired ordinariness, a prophetic common-sense.

The influence of his teaching has been so pervasive and far-reaching as to be strictly incalculable. The philosophers of the French Enlightenment all acknowledged Locke as their master, while the central British tradition of empiricism —the line of Berkeley, Hume, Mill, Russell, Ryle, Ayer— and the central American tradition of pragmatism are nothing if not Lockean. Rousseau and the makers of the American Revolution claimed to be Locke's disciples in politics, as did both the champions, and several of the critics, of the French Revolution. Locke's influence in spheres other than philosophy and politics was not less marked. Even literature, for which he had himself so limited a taste, was shaped by his teaching. Defoe and Sterne and Smollett are among those who invoke his name; not only Samuel Johnson and Henry Fielding, but equally Samuel Richardson and Jane Austen look at the world, and human conduct, in Lockean terms. Theirs is a world in which virtue is rewarded, in which cool self-love prevails, and where no-one, who is not foolish, seeks to penetrate the mysteries of the universe which lie beyond appearances. Not for them the kind of truth that is 'proved upon the pulses'; nor for them the attitude of those 'to whom the miseries of the world are misery and will not let them rest'. All that came with the Romantics; and if

romanticism in England was a reaction against anything,
it was a reaction—as William Blake was the first to realise—
against the *Weltanschauung* that men had learned from Locke.

VII

Locke did not despise the life of an *homme d'esprit* in
London society during the reign of William and Mary,
but the dirty air of the city made him ill. He had had
asthma for many years, and he now began to think he had
phthisis. He decided to accept a country retreat in Essex
which was offered him by Damaris Masham, the daughter
of Ralph Cudworth and wife of Sir Francis Masham, M.P.
Lady Masham and Locke had once exchanged love letters
and she was still very willing to lavish her care on him.
Locke remained a boarder in the Masham household until
his death in 1704 though, acting on the precept that an
intellectual ought not to live in 'a little goshen', he went
frequently to London. In 1696 his friend Sir John Somers,
the Whig leader and then virtual Prime Minister, gave him
the opportunity to become a Commissioner on the new
Board of Trade, and although he had refused several other
posts, and was in poorer health than he had ever been,
Locke accepted, installed William Popple as Secretary, and
for the next few years dominated everything the Board of
Trade did. He was seventy before he retired, to spend the
last two years of his life writing a commentary on the
New Testament.

One of the Board's duties was to investigate unemployment and the Poor Law. The plan Locke drew up for reform
in these fields is a revealing document. It shows that he
regarded poverty not as a misfortune but as a sign of moral
failure. Unemployment, Locke wrote, was due to 'the
relaxation of discipline and the corruption of manners' and
the first step 'towards setting the poor on work' should be

the closing of 'unnecessary alehouses'. Next, he recommended that any man found begging should, if under fifty,
be impressed for three years' naval service, or, if over fifty,
be sent to prison for three years' hard labour. Women
found begging, he suggested, might have lighter sentences,
but girls as well as boys under fourteen should be 'soundly
whipped'.

Locke also proposed methods for 'taking away the
pretence' that there was no work for the idle to do. First,
they should be put to work with private employers for
less than the usual rate of pay, under threat of impressment.
Secondly, pauper-schools should be set up in every parish
to enable both mothers and children to work productively.
As an economical diet for the children, Locke recommended
bread, supplemented in cold weather with 'a little water
gruel; for the same fire that warms the room may be made
use of to boil a pot of it'. By this means, 'computing all
the earnings of a child from three to fourteen years of age,
the nourishment and teaching of such a child during that
whole time will cost the parish nothing' instead of the
fifty or sixty pounds a year each pauper child was then
costing the parish under the existing Poor Law. Locke
added:

> Another advantage also of bringing children thus to a working
> school is that by this means they may be obliged to come constantly
> to church every Sunday . . . whereby they may be brought into
> some sense of religion . . .

Locke's 17th century contemporaries rejected the scheme,
but something very like it was adopted in the 19th century,
when Locke's Quaker biographer H. R. Fox Bourne,
wrote of it as 'excellent' and 'philanthropic'. Locke had a
curiously 'Victorian' attitude towards the lower orders.

In one of his books on monetary theory, he pointed out
that 'the labourers' share' of the national wealth "being
seldom more than a bare subsistence, never allows that
body of men time or opportunity to raise their thoughts

above that', or even to assert their interests against the rich unless "some common and great distress, uniting them in some universal ferment, makes them forget respect . . .' Locke did not mean with these words to suggest that labourers ought to have more than a bare subsistence, but rather that governments should ward off any 'common and great distress' which might make labourers forget the respect they owed their superiors.

Precisely because they had not more than a bare subsistence, working men were excluded from the full responsibilities and privileges of political society. For, as Locke said more than once, 'the great and chief end . . . of men's uniting into commonwealths and putting themselves under governments is the preservation of their property'. And although Locke said he used the word 'property' to mean 'that property which men have in their persons as well as their goods', he often also used the word in its more limited and familiar sense. The labourer's only 'goods' was his capacity to work, and the sale of that to an employer left him with nothing. If the labourer had therefore little material interest in the commonwealth, neither had he much rationality to contribute to it. 'The greatest part of mankind have not the leisure for learning and logic.' For these reasons Locke looked askance at 'numerous democracy'.

When William Penn told him about the social services he wished to introduce in Pennsylvania, Locke protested that such innovations would be inimical to the liberty of subjects. To sacrifice liberty for the sake of philanthropy seemed to Locke mistaken; the object might be good but the price was too high. If anyone had suggested sacrificing liberty for the sake of equality, Locke would have thought the sacrifice disastrous and the object foolish.

In the preface to the English edition of the first *Letter for Toleration* is a sentence which reads: 'Absolute liberty, just and true liberty, equal and impartial liberty is the thing we stand in need of.' Many people have supposed these words to be Locke's, and Lord King used them as an epigraph for his biography of the philosopher, but in fact the words were written by William Popple, the translator of the *Letter*.

Locke did *not* believe in absolute liberty, any more than he believed in absolute knowledge. Locke wanted as much knowledge as possible; and he thought the way to achieve as much as possible of each was to face the fact that both were limited and then to find out what the limitations were. Once men recognised that certain information could be had only in one or two fields, they could go on to acquire a great deal of probable information in other fields. Hence the seeming paradox of Locke's attempt in his *Human Understanding* to show how much men can know by demonstrating how little they can know.

Locke's political writings are less elaborately argued than his *Human Understanding*, but his technique is much the same. By demonstrating the liberty that men cannot have, Locke shows the liberty that men can have. The limits of liberty are set by the nature of political societies as such, by the necessity of protecting the life, property, and freedom of each from invasion by any other, and protecting the safety of all from common enemies. Once those limitations are understood, no other limitations need be borne, indeed no other limitations *should* be borne. Locke set men on the road to the greatest possible liberty by the method he used to set them on the road to the greatest possible knowledge—by teaching them the impossibility of the absolute.

LOCKE

A Select Bibliography

(Place of publication London, unless stated otherwise)

Bibliography:

> A BIBLIOGRAPHICAL INTRODUCTION TO THE STUDY OF JOHN LOCKE,
> by H. O. Christopherson. Oslo (1930)

Collected Editions and Selections:

> THE WORKS, 3 vols. (1714)
> — reprinted throughout the 18th century.
> THE WORKS, edited by Bishop Law, 4 vols. (1777)
> — the best collected edition.
> THE PHILOSOPHICAL WORKS, edited by J. A. St. John (1843)
> THE EDUCATIONAL WRITINGS, edited by J. W. Adamson. Cambridge (1912)
> — revised edition, 1922.
> TREATISE OF CIVIL GOVERNMENT AND A LETTER CONCERNING TOLERATION, edited by J. W. Gough. Oxford (1946)
> — also in *The Social Contract* (World's Classics), edited by E. Barker, Oxford (1946)
> LOCKE AND LIBERTY: A SELECTION FROM THE WORKS OF JOHN LOCKE, compiled with an Introduction by M. Salvadori (1960)
> — the editor's preface contains some points of interest.

Separate Works:

> EPISTOLA DE TOLERANTIA AD CLARISSIMUM VIRUM . . . Tergou (1689)
> — English translation, 1689; edited by H. Morley, 1889.
> TWO TREATISES OF GOVERNMENT (1690)
> — edited by H. Morley, 1884; edited by W. F. Carpenter, 1924, in Everyman's Library. The definitive, critical edition of P. Laslett, Cambridge, 1960, which reproduces the original text and adds an introduction and commentary, revolutionises many long-standing views concerning the author's intentions.
> AN ESSAY CONCERNING HUMAN UNDERSTANDING (1690)
> — enlarged, 1694 and 1700. A two-volume edition edited by A. C. Fraser, Oxford, 1894, was prepared after collation with four editions published in Locke's lifetime, and with the French version by Coste (1700) done under Locke's supervision. See also *An Early Draft of Locke's Essay*, Oxford, 1936, edited by R. I. Aaron and J. Gibb from one of the three surviving MSS.

35

A SECOND LETTER CONCERNING TOLERATION (1690)

SOME CONSIDERATIONS OF THE CONSEQUENCES OF THE LOWERING OF INTEREST, AND RAISING THE VALUE OF MONEY (1692)

A THIRD LETTER FOR TOLERATION (1692)

— the Letters on Toleration have several times been printed together, notably by A. Millar, 1765, and A. Murray in 1870.

SOME THOUGHTS CONCERNING EDUCATION (1693)

— enlarged, 1695; edited by R. H. Quick, Cambridge, 1880. The most useful edition is in the *Educational Writings*, edited by J. W. Adamson, 1912. (See *Collected Editions and Selections*, above).

FURTHER CONSIDERATIONS CONCERNING RAISING THE VALUE OF MONEY (1695)

THE REASONABLENESS OF CHRISTIANITY AS DELIVERED IN THE SCRIPTURES (1695)

A VINDICATION OF THE REASONABLENESS OF CHRISTIANITY, FROM MR. EDWARDS'S REFLECTIONS (1695)

A SECOND VINDICATION OF THE REASONABLENESS OF CHRISTIANITY (1697)

— the best later edition is in *Sacred Classics* edited by R. Cottesnole and H. Stebbing, vol. xxv, 1836.

A LETTER TO THE RIGHT REVEREND LORD BISHOP OF WORCESTER, CONCERNING SOME PASSAGES RELATING TO MR. LOCKE'S ESSAY ON HUMAN UNDERSTANDING (1697)

MR. LOCKE'S REPLY TO THE RIGHT REVEREND LORD BISHOP OF WORCESTER'S ANSWER TO HIS LETTER (1697)

MR. LOCKE'S REPLY TO THE RIGHT REVEREND LORD BISHOP OF WORCESTER'S ANSWER TO HIS SECOND LETTER (1698)

A PARAPHRASE AND NOTES ON THE EPISTLE OF ST. PAUL TO THE GALATIANS (1705)

POSTHUMOUS WORKS (1706)

— contains 'Of the Conduct of Understanding'; edited by T. Fowler, Oxford, 1901.

REMAINS (1714)

AN ESSAY CONCERNING THE UNDERSTANDING, KNOWLEDGE, OPINION, AND ASSENT, edited by B. Rand. Harvard (1931)

LOCKE'S TRAVELS IN FRANCE 1675–1679, edited by J. Lough. Cambridge (1953)

— Locke's diaries of his French travels published for the first time.

ESSAYS ON THE LAWS OF NATURE, edited by W. von Leyden. Oxford (1954)
— the Latin text, with a translation and introduction. This is an extremely early text of Locke's, discovered among the Lovelace papers by the editor, whose introduction is of exceptional interest.

Correspondence:

SOME FAMILIAR LETTERS BETWEEN MR. LOCKE AND SEVERAL OF HIS FRIENDS (1708)

ORIGINAL LETTERS OF JOHN LOCKE, ALGERNON SYDNEY AND LORD SHAFTESBURY, edited by T. Forster (1830)

LETTRES INÉDITES DE JOHN LOCKE, [edited by] H. Ollion. The Hague (1912)

THE CORRESPONDENCE OF JOHN LOCKE AND EDWARD CLARKE, edited by B. Rand. Oxford (1927)

Note: A definitive edition of Locke's letters is being prepared by E. S. De Beer for the Clarendon Press.

Some Bibliographical and Critical Studies:

LA PHILOSPOHIE DE LOCKE, par V. Cousin. Paris (1819)

THE LIFE OF JOHN LOCKE WITH EXTRACTS FROM HIS CORRESPONDENCE, JOURNALS AND COMMONPLACE BOOKS, by Lord King. 2 vols. (1829)

THE LIFE OF ANTHONY ASHLEY COOPER, FIRST EARL OF SHAFTESBURY, by W. D. Christie. 2 vols. (1871)

THE LIFE OF JOHN LOCKE, by H. R. F. Bourne. 2 vols. (1876)
— this substantial Victorian work has not lost its utility, despite later discoveries.

LOCKE'S THEORY OF KNOWLEDGE, by J. Gibson. Cambridge (1917)
— a particularly helpful guide to the *Essay*.

THE MORAL AND POLITICAL PHILOSOPHY OF JOHN LOCKE, by S. Lamprecht. New York (1918)

LOCKE, BERKELEY AND HUME, by C. R. Morris. Oxford (1931)

THE DEVELOPMENT OF RELIGIOUS TOLERATION IN ENGLAND, by W. K. Jordan (1932)

JOHN LOCKE, by N. K. Smith. Manchester (1933)

JOHN LOCKE: TERCENTENARY ADDRESSES, by G. Ryle. Oxford (1933)

THE FIRST EARL OF SHAFTESBURY, by L. F. Brown. New York (1933)

JOHN LOCKE, by R. I. Aaron. Oxford (1937)
— the second edition, 1955, of this, the best-known modern commentary on Locke's philosophy, has been brought into line with recent research into the history of the *Essay Concerning Human Understanding*.

THE RELIGIOUS OPINIONS OF MILTON, LOCKE AND NEWTON, by H. McLachlan. Manchester (1941)

JOHN LOCKE'S POLITICAL PHILOSOPHY: EIGHT STUDIES, by J. W. Gough. Oxford (1950)
— stimulating, sometimes controversial, interpretations of Locke's political theory.

RALPH CUDWORTH, by J. A. Passmore. Cambridge (1951)

JOHN LOCKE, by D. J. O'Connor (1952)
— an up-to-date and useful commentary, published by Penguin Books as a paper-back 'Pelican'.

LES RELATIONS INTELLECTUELLES DE LOCKE AVEC LA FRANCE, [edited by] G. Bonno. Berkeley, Cal. (1955)

JOHN LOCKE: A BIOGRAPHY, by M. Cranston (1957)
— this biography is largely based on the Earl of Lovelace's inherited collection of Locke MSS, which was acquired by the Bodleian Library, partly by purchase, in 1948, and partly by gift (from Paul Mellon) in 1960. The Mellon gift also included over 600 volumes from Locke's library, many of them with Locke's autograph marginalia.